D1539530

GREEN GENERAL CONTRACTOR

Published in the United States of America by Cherry Lake Publishing
Ann Arbor, Michigan
www.cherrylakepublishing.com

Content Adviser: Doug Selby, Meadowlark Builders, Ann Arbor, Michigan
Reading Adviser: Marla Conn MS, Ed., Literacy specialist, Read-Ability, Inc.

Photo Credits: © SpeedKingz/Shutterstock, cover, 1; © Joe Ferrer | Dreamstime.com; © Len Collection / Alamy Stock Photo;
© Noradoa/Shutterstock, 8; 11tk; © Marcin-linfernum/Shutterstock, 12; © shironosov/istock, 14; © Imagesbybarbara/istock, 17;
© Meadowlark Builders, 18, 20; © Greg Epperson | Dreamstime.com; © bikeriderlondon/Shutterstock, 24; © Linfernum |
Dreamstime.com - Ecological Modern Building Of Library Photo; © Shutterstock/Mana Photo, 26;
© LUCARELLI TEMISTOCLE/Shutterstock, 28

Library of Congress Cataloging-in-Publication Data
Names: Labrecque, Ellen, author.
Title: Green general contractor / Ellen Labrecque.
Other titles: 21st century skills library. Cool careers.
Description: Ann Arbor, MI : Cherry Lake Publishers, [2016] |
Series: Cool careers | Audience: Grades 4 to 6. |
    Includes bibliographical references.
Identifiers: LCCN 2015049649| ISBN 9781634710633 (hardcover) |
    ISBN 9781634712613 (pbk.) | ISBN 9781634711623 (pdf) | ISBN 9781634713603 (ebook)
Subjects: LCSH: Sustainable construction—Vocational guidance—Juvenile literature. |
    Sustainable buildings—Design and construction—Juvenile literature. | Contractors—Juvenile literature.
Classification: LCC TH880 .L33 2016 | DDC 690.023—dc23
LC record available at http://lccn.loc.gov/2015049649

Cherry Lake Publishing would like to acknowledge the work of the Partnership for 21st Century Learning.
Please visit www.p21.org for more information.

Printed in the United States of America
Corporate Graphics

ABOUT THE AUTHOR

Ellen Labrecque is a freelance writer living in Yardley, Pennsylvania. Previously, she was a senior editor at *Sports Illustrated Kids*. Ellen loves to travel and then learn about new places and people she can write about in her books.

TABLE OF CONTENTS

Going Green

On May 4, 2007, a tornado swept through Greensburg, Kansas, destroying 90 percent of the town's buildings. Roofs were torn from homes. Fierce winds ripped trees out of the ground and threw them through walls. Bricks and other rubble dotted the streets. This tornado is still one of the strongest on record. It left 1,400 people homeless. Greensburg lay in ruin. The community decided to rebuild in a new way.

Today, close to 10 years after the tornado, Greensburg has been reborn into a totally green town, with many LEED-certified buildings. LEED stands for Leadership in Energy and Environmental Design. It became the first city in the United States to use all LED (light-emitting diode) streetlights. LED lights use energy in a more efficient way. And, most importantly,

Solar panels are one way to make a building greener.

all the electricity used in the city is produced by the wind, which means it is 100 percent renewable.

LEED-certified buildings use less energy and less water. They are built with sustainable and recycled materials whenever possible. There are many reasons to be interested in green buildings. According to the Green Building Council, buildings—commercial and public buildings and homes—use around 40 percent of the country's energy. Green buildings greatly reduce energy consumption and water use. This saves natural resources.

Since the tornado, Greensburg has remodeled many of its buildings.

The people of Greensburg now live in homes built by green contractors. The well-**insulated** homes cost less to heat and to cool. They are made of recycled wood. Lawns are filled with native plants instead of grass. These plants are adapted to the environment and require less water than traditional grass. Green contractors installed Energy Star–rated appliances to help save gas and electricity. This means the appliances use much less energy than the limit given by the government.

Life and Career Skills

The Green Schools Alliance is an international organization that encourages schools all over the world to go as green as possible. It teaches schools how to use less energy and water, as well as how to connect more with nature. The alliance includes more than 3,000 schools in over 37 different countries. Do you want your school to join? Check out greenschoolsalliance.org for more information!

Buildings that are powered by wind save on electricity costs.

Greensburg is one of the greenest towns in America, but it is not the only place using green contractors. A city does not need to be completely rebuilt to "go green." Green contractors can **remodel** homes, businesses, and public buildings to make them more comfortable, more energy efficient, and healthier for the people who use them.

Throughout the world, interest in green buildings is growing. Some businesses use **wind turbines** or gas from landfills to help power factories. Green schools, such as the Academy for Global Citizenship in Chicago, Illinois, have saved thousands of dollars a year in energy costs. The academy gets much of its energy from solar panels installed on the roof.

In the town of Corvallis, Oregon, residents compete to see who can use the lowest amount of energy in their homes. Green builders have built two LEED-certified buildings, and more are on the way.

These green towns, buildings, and schools can help improve the planet's health and save resources. Every one of these projects needs a green **general contractor** to supervise it.

CHAPTER 2

What a Green Contractor Does

A general contractor organizes building projects. He or she is responsible for making sure the work is done correctly. He or she also manages the workers who do the actual building. A contractor's job begins with the **blueprints**, or plans for a building. It usually ends when the building is finished, but a contractor may be called back if something needs to be fixed after the building is completed.

Contractors start a project by getting the architect's blueprints. Blueprints show every part of the job, from walls and windows to plumbing and heating. They also show details for each floor as well as the outsides of the building. Everything is measured precisely.

Contractors do not do all the **construction** work themselves.

With detailed blueprints, a contractor can feel confident about the project.

They hire trade workers such as landscapers, electricians, and plumbers. Each trade worker gives the contractor an estimate for the cost of the job. For example, a plumber gives the contractor an estimate for the pipes, drains, and other parts of the plumbing system. The estimate includes the cost of the building materials and the plumber's labor. Once a contractor knows what each job will cost, he or she can determine a total cost for constructing the building. He or she then makes a bid on the project. A bid is a contractor's offer to provide labor and materials for a certain price.

In a rain garden, rainwater naturally flows down to reach the plants.

General contractors must be well organized and schedule their projects carefully. They also need to work well with people. A building project often has several different trade workers on the job at the same time. As parts of buildings are finished, contractors call in other trade workers to begin their jobs. For example, the electrician must finish wiring the building before the contractor brings the carpenter in to finish the woodwork. Landscapers don't start working until the building is nearly finished.

A green building does more than just **conserve** resources. It is also safer for the environment. "Green building is a way of addressing energy issues and indoor air quality," says Bill Browning, a green building consultant. "It makes for healthier and less-expensive places to live and work."

David Arkin, a green architect, agrees. He notes the importance of buildings that can heat and cool themselves. "Ecological designs can be beautiful and be a part of the **mainstream**," he says.

21st Century Content

One of the latest trends in green design is a rain garden. Rain gardens are designed to absorb and capture the rain. They may have a wall around them to prevent runoff. Water runoff can cause erosion, water pollution, and flooding. The plants in these gardens are specially chosen for their deep roots, which help them take in the water. Want to learn more about saving the rain? Go to http://savetherain.us.

Future green general contractors need very strong math skills.

Becoming a green general contractor requires additional education and experience. High school students can prepare by taking math, science, and computer technology classes. In college, future contractors should study construction management, architecture, or **civil engineering**. They should also take classes on environmental science, physics, and mathematics.

Each state has its own laws about who can be a contractor. In some states, a contractor must pass a test to earn a **license**. Contractors are tested on their knowledge of the trades and on other subjects, such as insurance and safety. Contractors usually must pay exam and licensing fees.

Most new college graduates in this field start by working for large construction companies. They estimate building costs. They manage small jobs or purchase materials for larger jobs. This work experience helps new workers in the construction industry move on to jobs with more responsibility.

Meet a Green Contractor

Traditional contractors and green contractors differ in many ways. Green contractors make more choices based on the environment and use more green building materials. Many green general contractors work to educate the public about more environmentally safe ways to build.

Thomas G. Wells is a green remodeler who has worked in green construction for 30 years. His work focuses on making sure a person's home is energy efficient. "Many homes in the U.S. just leak air," Wells explains. "There are cracks and crevices that blow the air out of the house."

Wells's company does energy audits on houses. Audits are a series of tests to see how much air the house is losing. After the audit is done, Wells and his crew go to work. They seal the

Contractors need to know how to fix common building problems, like leaks.

house's cracks and holes to make it a lot more energy efficient. They use spray foam insulation, which helps keep the home warm in winter and cool in summer.

Wells also does a lot of public speaking to promote the benefits of green building. He is a member of the Citizens' Climate Lobby, which is an organization trying to get the U.S. government to address climate change.

For Wells, becoming a green contractor seemed like the right thing to do. He's always been concerned about the environment, "and green building seemed the perfect way"

A green house doesn't disturb plants or animals that live nearby.

to help address his concerns.

"We all have an obligation as humans to try and take better care of our earth," he says. "Green building is one of the ways to do this."

Green builders don't just worry about the building. They also consider the environment of the building site. They try to avoid damaging natural **habitats**. They try to maintain green spaces such as forestlands, meadows, and prairies. People who live and work in green buildings enjoy better air quality and fewer potentially harmful chemicals.

21st Century Content

Have you ever watched a house being built? It seems like there is always a lot of trash around the building site, right? There is. An estimated 8,000 pounds (3,629 kilograms) of garbage is generated during construction of a 2,000-square-foot (186 square-meter) home. The good news? Green builders don't let these scraps go to waste. They recycle old drywall into new drywall. They take the cardboard and the packaging to paper mills to recycle. The scrap metal is shipped and eventually melted down and reused. Building green means nothing ever goes to waste!

Green general contractors often use recycled materials.

It is important for green contractors to use green materials. Insulation can be produced from recycled newspaper and wood pulp. Flooring can be made from recycled rubber. The latest lightbulbs use less energy. Special toilets, sinks, and water fountains use less water. This helps keep energy costs down. Green building materials should not cause allergies or contain toxins. Researchers are often discovering new green materials. Green contractors must keep up with the latest products.

In the long-term, green general contractors can build a green home for about the same cost as a regular home. At first, the materials will be more expensive since they are higher quality. Other green features, such as wind turbines or solar panels, also add to the cost of a building. But sometimes they generate more power than the building's owner can use. The extra power can be sold back to the **utility** company. This means green power sources can eventually pay for themselves.

Most green contractors earn a good salary. It depends on many things, including the size and type of projects the contractor works on. Some earn more than $100,000. Some earn about half that much. Many contractors also earn bonuses. Green contractors work hard for their money.

CHAPTER 4

The Future Is Bright with Green

The future of green building couldn't be brighter. In fact, the pace of green building is now faster than the overall construction industry growth! Interest in lowering energy costs and preserving natural resources is growing. Scientists warn about global warming and greenhouse gases. Green building alone cannot solve these problems, but it is the best place to start.

Both the U.S. Green Building Council and the National Association of Home Builders offer classes and certification for green building methods. Students can take part in seminars, join a workshop, and study online. To become a Certified Green Professional or a LEED AP (accredited professional), a contractor must pass a difficult test. Despite the demands, there are nearly 3,000 people in the United States who are certified green

Green buildings are more common now than ever before.

contractors today. More are always needed!

The advantages of green building are clear. Going green uses recycled or **reclaimed** products to conserve raw materials. It reduces or recycles waste during the building process. Green buildings use less energy and less water. They make use of renewable energy sources such as solar power or wind power. Finally, green building produces a long-lasting, quality product.

Green buildings were once an expensive luxury. Green materials, architects, and contractors were hard to find. Today, the market for green building is booming. According to experts,

Many people want to remodel their homes to be greener.

Solar panels are becoming more common.

green construction is expected to outgrow traditional construction by 2020.

In 2015, more than 4.3 million people already lived and worked in LEED-certified buildings. This number is only expected to grow. By 2019, LEED buildings are projected to save $2.4 billion in energy costs and create more than 2.3 million more jobs in the United States! More and more people are realizing that going green can save them money in the long run while also helping the planet.

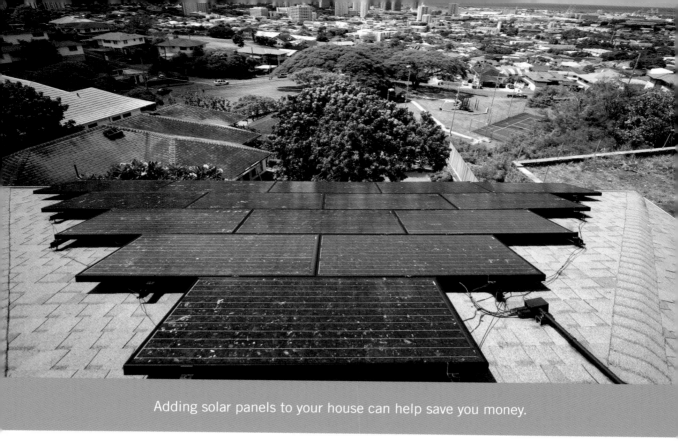

Adding solar panels to your house can help save you money.

Federal, local, and state governments are also planning for a green future. The U.S. government offers tax breaks to builders of new green homes. Tax breaks are available to those who remodel to meet green standards, too. The U.S. government has adopted new green guidelines for building and remodeling public structures. Cities and towns are adding green building codes to reduce the use of energy and water. To meet these new standards, many people will hire green contractors. Today's construction workers are learning new skills, using innovative materials, and finding jobs that did not previously exist.

Saving energy is a big part of green construction. Green contractors find ways to use renewable sources of energy instead of **fossil fuels**. According to the Associated General Contractors of America's "Building a Green Future" plan, "Across the country, contractors are finding new work installing wind turbines, installing **geothermal** heating and cooling systems, 'planting' solar farms, and connecting new sources of power to existing [power] grids."

21st Century Content

In 2015, the Web site NerdWallet ranked America's greenest cities. Their top 5 are:
1. Honolulu, Hawaii (for its great air quality and lots of solar energy)
2. Washington, D.C. (for its excellent public transportation system, meaning that fewer people drive cars)
*3. Arlington, Virginia (for having **commuters** who walk and good air quality)*
4. San Francisco, California (for having commuters who walk and lots of solar energy)
5. Miami, Florida (for having commuters who carpool and great air quality)

The more common solar panels become, the cheaper they will be to buy.

The push for more green energy is really working. The solar industry has been adding jobs 10 times faster than any other occupation. And since the beginning of 2010, the average cost of a solar electric system has dropped by 50 percent. This makes solar energy even more affordable for everyone. It's never been a more popular time to go green—especially when building is involved!

21st Century Content

Why should everybody go with green building instead of regular construction? Here's why: According to the Environmental Protection Agency, traditional, non-green buildings in the United States account for roughly:
- 36 percent of the nation's total energy use
- 12 percent of its potable water consumption
- 65 percent of its total electricity consumption
- 30 percent of its carbon dioxide (greenhouse gas) emissions
- 30 percent of its waste output (136 million tons annually)

Think About It

Do you go to a green school? If not, you can't change the way the school is built. But are there other ways you can help your school go green?

The famous architect Frank Lloyd Wright said, "Buildings too are the children of the Earth and the Sun." What do you think he meant by that? Do you think a green general contractor feels the same way?

The homes in the United States are getting bigger. The average home today has over 2,600 square feet (241.5 sq m). This is more than 60 percent larger on average than homes were in 1973. Do you think bigger homes are more or less energy efficient than smaller homes? Why or why not?

For More Information

BOOKS

Amsel, Sheri. *365 Ways to Live Green for Kids: Saving the Environment at Home, School, or at Play—Every Day!* Avon, MA: Adams Media, 2009.

Javna, John. *The New 50 Simple Things Kids Can Do to Save the Earth*. Kansas City, MO: Andrews McMeel Publishing, 2009.

Kirk, Ellen. *Human Footprint*. Washington, DC: National Geographic Children's Books, 2011.

WEB SITES

Children of the Earth United
www.childrenoftheearth.org/green-building-sustainable-homes/introduction-to
-building-green-homes.htm
Watch a video about how green contractors work with nature when they build new structures.

The Green Schools Alliance
www.greenschoolsalliance.org
Learn more about how schools can go green.

GLOSSARY

blueprints (BLOO-prints) detailed plans for a structure

civil engineering (SIV-uhl en-juh-NEER-ing) designing and constructing public building projects such as roads

commuters (kuh-MYOO-turz) people who travel some distances to work or school each day, usually by car, bus, train, or walking

conserve (kuhn-SURV) to use less

construction (kuhn-STRUHK-shuhn) the business of building permanent structures

fossil fuels (FAH-suhl FYOO-uhls) coal, oil, or natural gas, formed from the remains of prehistoric plants and animals

general contractor (JEN-ur-uhl KAHN-trakt-ur) a person or company who organizes and supervises building projects

geothermal (jee-oh-THUR-muhl) heat from beneath the surface of the earth

habitats (HAB-ih-tats) the places and conditions in which things live and grow

insulated (IN-suh-layt-id) covered with material to prevent hot (or cool) air from escaping

license (LYE-suhns) a legal permission to do something

mainstream (MAYN-streem) things that are thought to be normal or typical

reclaimed (rih-KLAYMD) something obtained from a waste product

remodel (ree-MAH-duhl) rebuild or renovate

utility (yoo-TIL-ih-tee) a basic service supplied to a community, such as telephone, water, gas or electricity

wind turbines (WIND TUR-buhnz) machines that generate energy from wind

INDEX